Stand Up
and
Tell Them Some More

by Crawford Howard, Billy Ritchie,
Seamus Lavery and Bill Nesbitt

Edited by Liz Weir
Illustrations by Doreen McBride

ADARE PRESS
White Gables
Ballymoney Hill
Banbridge
Telephone: (08206) 23782

© 1992 Crawford Howard, Billy Ritchie, Seamus
Lavery and Bill Nesbitt
Published by Adare Press
Typeset by December Publications
Printed by Banbridge Chronicle

ISBN 0 9516686 4 1

Stand Up and Tell Them Some More

Stories in verse have always been very much part of traditional social life in Ireland and although perhaps more popular in days when people attended guest teas and ceilidhs rather than watching television and video, they have continued to survive as an art form. Whenever people gather together to enjoy an evening's "crack" there is sure to be someone who neither sings nor plays an instrument but who can stand up and deliver a recitation. This collection aims to provide new additions to the repertoire.

The first collection of verse, "Stand Up And Tell Them" was a best seller within Northern Ireland. Amongst the writers featured was Crawford Howard, whose wry looks at life in Northern Ireland proved popular with people of all age groups and backgrounds. This volume contains some more of Crawford's work together with additional pieces by Billy Ritchie who also has a reputation for acute observation of the Ulster condition. These two writers are joined by Seamus Lavery. He frequently performs in public and his verse has been enjoyed by radio listeners who jammed the telephone lines in the BBC seeking copies to share with their friends.

Bill Nesbitt is the fourth member of this quartet. His verse appears each week in "The Sunday World," has been broadcast frequently and is often performed in public at storytelling events.

The aim of this volume, like that of "Stand Up And Tell Them" is to encourage people to read, or recite, these pieces ALOUD at gatherings of friends or families. The feedback from the previous book is that people did just that and it is our hope that more and more people will be encouraged to share these verses as well and that they will enjoy themselves at the same time.

Liz Weir
Ahoghill
August 1992

Contents

Crawford Howard

And she disappeared down like a bloody great mole!

Crawford Howard lives in Belfast and is well known as a musician as well as a storyteller. His verses have received acclaim following their performance on radio and television and he has produced two tapes, "The Diagonal Steamtrap" and "The Slopin' Beauty." His success has left him "agog with apathy" (to quote his own words!) and he continues to observe the world with his own quirky sense of humour!

Maggie Kilmartin's Trip to Australia

Air : The Blackthorn Stick

Now Maggie Kilmartin from Ballygomartin was fond of her grub
    and as fat as a pig,
For drinkin' and atin' she couldn't be baten from Belfast to Bangor,
    from Cork to Conlig.
Her enormous figure got bigger and bigger
Her weight was in excess of eighty-five stone!
She twisted her ankle one night on the Shankill
And said, "Holy Jesus! I'll never get home!"

There was a terrible sound when oul' Meg hit the ground
And out of the belfreys flew hundreds of bats
The noise it was shockin' and buildings was rockin'
From Tennent Street till the Unity Flats
Then the polis said, "Here! We must get the street clear!
Thon bomb must have weighed more than two hundred pounds!"
Then a fella came runnin' and said, "Don't be funny!
It's Maggie Kilmartin has fell on the ground!"

Now they all tried to lift her, but nothin' could shift her.
She lay like a big stranded whale in the street
The traffic was slowin' and the horns was all blowin'
The polis at last had admitted defeat
So a plan was concerted, the traffic diverted
The polis admitted they hadn't a clue
They said, "This is barmy, we'll send for the army,
We'll see if them fellas 'll know what to do!"

Now the army soon came with a massive great crane
And said, "We'll soon shift her, on that you can swear."
So they started the engine an' pullin' and winchin'
The wheels of the crane went straight up in the air
Then a soldier said, "Maisie! Do you see what I see?
She's sinking right down in a ruddy great 'ole!"
And under oul' Mag the ground started to sag
And she disappeared down like a bloody great mole!

Now as they all feared Maggie disappeared
And they all gathered round to see where she had gone
An' amidst roars of laughter the crane follied after
Wi' polis an' army an' all hangin' on!
They said, "It's a failure, she's away to Australia!
You better give in and give Sydney a ring
For if they can't reject her at least they'll expect her,
To arrive unannounced is a terrible thing!"

With puffin' an' blowin' oul Maggie kept goin'.
An' found at last she was gettin' too warm
She said, "This is shockin', I've burnt my good stockins!
If I had of knew, I would not have put them on!"
But slowly and surely she got to Kalgoorlie
The Australians stood round as the ground it did crack,
And they said, "This old geezer's got no flamin' visa!"
So they hit her a kick and sent her straight back.

Now Meg went back down through the hole in the ground
And soon she was back in the heat and the smoke.
Says she, "This is no go! I feel like a yo-yo!
The heat and the stour here would near make you boke!"
But the funny thing was like, whatever the cause like,
The way these things happens beyond you nor me
She burnt her good sweater but her ankle got better
She leapt out in the Shankill as fit as a flea!

Now my sad tale of woe now, has not long to go now,
For Maggie decided that she would get thin
They gave her a diet, she thought she would try it
So she went and threw all her grub in the bin.
She got wee-er and wee-er till you could hardly see her
She could almost walk through a crack in a door
For want of good 'atin' she slipped through a gratin'
And never was seen in the Shankill no more!

Crawford Howard

The White House Concert

Jimmy Johnston was a young Belfast musician
The instruments he played I just can't tell.
He nearly deeved his grannie when he played the oul' piannie,
And his oul' lad said he played the goat as well.
He played trumpets, he played trombones and tin whistles
And to hear him on the bagpipes was a treat.
He could play you fifty tunes on a pair of oul' tin spoons
That he picked up from the chipper down the street.

His fame soon spread throughout the nation,
He was playin' somewhere different every day,
But the pinnacle of fame was when the summons came
To go and play out in the U.S.A.
When he heard the news Jim says, "You must be jokin'!
I'm sure the Yanks don't want to hear ME play!"
But his agent says, "No geggin! You're to play for Ronald Reagan
In the White House, on the twenty third of May!"

So Jimmy hurried home to do his packing,
(A carry-out of fifty cans of beer
And his cleanest dirty vest, for he had to look his best
When appearing at the function of the year.)
He was met by President Reagan at the air-port,
An' he shouted, "Bout ye Jimmy? Can you wait?
I'm just loadin' up this van with these missiles for Iran
But I'll see ye in five minutes at the gate!"

So they climbed into the Presidential 'limo',
With the trumpets and trombones in the boot,
An' Mr. Reagan muttered, "Dammit! Isn't that the bloody limit!
I've got grease from them oul' missiles on my suit!
I toul them all we never should have bothered
I knew that muggins here would get the blame!
An' as for thon oul' Ayatollah, ye couldn't trust that fella
Them foreigners is all the flippin' same!"

When they landed at the White House it was 'hivin'
-Film stars and politicians by the score-
An' downstairs the bar was buzzin' with musicians by the dozen
An' Frank Sinatra houlin' up the door.
There was grub enough to feed a dozen armies.
There was turkey, pastie suppers, ham and cake.
An' wee Jimmy got 'tore in' for although the lad was thin
He could fairly shovel grub intil his 'bake'.

He was tearin' through his second pastie supper
When the M.C. shouted, "Jimmy lad! You're on!"
An' wee Jimmy almost choked, in fact he nearly 'boked' -
But he quickly grabbed his trumpet and a scone.
He swallied down two chips an' put the trumpet till his lips
Intendin' for to give it all he'd got,
But the trumpet made a noise that did not make his heart rejoice
And the audience sat rooted to the spot!

FOR HE'D GOT A BIT OF CRUMPET IN HIS TRUMPET
IT WOULD NOT SHIFT NO MATTER HOW HE BLEW
AND WITH A BIT OF CRUMPET IN YOUR TRUMPET
THERE'S VERY LITTLE ANYONE CAN DO!

But wee Jimmy was never known to be a quitter.
He dropped the clogged-up trumpet on the deck,
An' he muttered, "That's the limit!" as he dug inside his simmet
An' pulled out an oul' tin whistle by the neck.
He thought, "I'll give the audience a treat now!
I'll get them on their feet with jigs and reels!"
But the whistle wouldn't whistle - sure all it did was fistle-
And emit the most peculiar shrieks and squeals!

FOR HE'D GOT A BIT OF GRISTLE IN HIS WHISTLE.
IT WOULD NOT SHIFT NO MATTER HOW HE BLEW
AND WITH A BIT OF GRISTLE IN YOUR WHISTLE
THERE'S VERY LITTLE ANYONE CAN DO!

Now wee Jim was goin' frantic with frustration,
The audience began to shout and yell.
And several alcoholics stood up and shouted, "Rubbish!"
And Jimmy thought, "Yez all can go to Hell!"
Then he thought, "I'll have a go on thon piana!"
An' he tuk a wild buck-lep across the floor,
But when he tried to play it nearly turned him grey
For such a noise you never heard before!

A BANANA HAD GOT STUCK IN THE PIANA
THE STRINGS HAD GOT ENTANGLED IN THE SKIN
AN' WITH BANANA STUCK IN YOUR PIANA
THERE'S NO WAY THAT YOU'RE EVER GOIN' TO WIN!

Now that was Jimmy's dream of stardom ended
He never made it big on old Broadway
But he always checks for gristle before he lifts a whistle
An' he has a drink before he starts to play.
He's playin' drums in the Salvation Army
And he muses on his sad and mournful plight,
But bananas and pianas and crumpet in his trumpet
Still give him nightmares every flamin' night!

Crawford Howard

P.R.

This poem may be sung to the Air "Father O'Flynn".

You may talk of your lords and yer oul' aristocracy,
Bishops, an' clergy, an' that oul hypocrisy,
We are the party that stands for democracy,
An Jimmy McStravick's the man for yer vote!
Jimmy was never in Church in his life.
Spent every Sunday in batin' the wife.
Still in reality, he has the quality
Jimmy McStravick's the man for yer vote!

Now if Jimmy gets in there'll be great joviality,
Drink will be cheap and much better in quality,
The whole City Hall will be filled with joviality,
So Jimmy McStravick's the man for yer vote!
Pubs will be open from daylight till dawn,
Ye'll never go home till yer money's all gone,
For mirth and for frolic, for drinks alcoholic,
For songs diabolical Jimmy's yer man.

Do the Unionists know if they're comin' or goin'?
Oul' Faulkner's determined to make a good showin'
Bill Craig and the rest are all puffin' and blowin'
But Jimmy McStravick's the man for your vote.
Then there's oul' Fitt and the S.D.L.P.
The Loyalist Front an' the V.U.P.P.
All met with defiance from thon oul' Alliance,
But Jimmy McStravick's the fella for me.

Ye see this proportional representation,
The like of it's never been seen in the Nation
Yer votin' slip's like a quadratic equation
But Jimmy McStravick's the man for yer vote!
Sez Jim, "Do they think that the voters is fools?"
To fill in yer slip is like doin' the pools
Perm eight from eleven or plan twenty-seven
But Jimmy McStravick will stick to the rules!"

11

Says a fella to Jimmy, "Yer no politician!
We want Ulster restored to its former position!"
Sez Jim, "Do you think I'm a bloody magician?"
But Jimmy McStravick's the man for yer vote!
So let Jimmy's supporters in thousands be seen
We'll show Mr. Whitewash it's business we mean!
An end to corruption! Let's vote for disruption!
McStravicks for havoc! And God save the Queen!

Crawford Howard

Billy Ritchie

Billy Ritchie is now well known as a performer at storytelling events, having been a featured teller at the 1991 Scottish Storytelling Festival as well as at numerous local sessions. He has appeared on Ulster Television and has many broadcasts to his credit, including Radio Ulster's "Gift of the Gab" series. He lives in Gilford, County Down, where he continues to write verse which is ideal for reading aloud.

The Orthopaedic Bed

A certain lady whom I know,
Was out one morning shovelling snow.
She slipped and took an awful crack,
Then found that she had strained her back.
Some friends came by and quickly bore
Her to the doctor's open door,
But though that door was extra wide
They couldn't bundle her inside.
It seemed that it just wasn't on,
The problem bein' the shape she'd gone,
But eventually they got her there
By handling her like a big armchair.
The doctor took a thorough look
And wrote some notes down in a book.
Then solemnly to her proclaimed,
"I think you've got some muscles strained,
The only cure for which I know,
A hard bed, use a month or so,
I can't commend a whole lot more
Except you try a concrete floor."
She didn't give him any thanks
For his suggestion, "Lie on planks!"
So, from that place straight home she went
Disgruntled and her patience spent,
Did nothing until someone said,
"Why not an orthopaedic bed?"
She first declined, then thought not why
Give the infernal thing a try?
She ordered one, it came at three
Delivered by the N.I.C.
That night she got in for a sleep
Still thinking she'd be counting sheep,
But very much to her suprise
She never stirred until sunrise
And further to her great delight
She found her back was now alright!
Her friends were very much amazed
As over tea the bed she praised,
Told all and sundry what she'd found

And so the story got around.
Soon people that were passing by
Would drop in to give it a try
And as the story travelled far
They came by bus and motor car.
What doctors couldn't understand
Was its uniqueness in the land,
While football players, men of sport
Came all their injuries to sort.
Queues formed in everlasting line
While people tried five at a time
Soon many wondrous cures were claimed
The bed throughout the land was famed.
People came away with smiles
The roads were blocked with cars for miles.
The whole thing was miraculish
It seemed they'd just to lie and wish.
An oul lad hobbled off the street
And cured the bunions on his feet.
An oul girl tried it for her plan
It seems she wished to trap a man.
And all the time the story spread
About this wondrous magic bed.
Contending with the crowds increase
Required three hundred traffic police,
With traffic jams on every beat
And riots breaking in the street.
The whole thing had got out of hand,
Such stress the lady could not stand.
She thought, "I must get out of it,"
And that night did a moonlight flit.
I can't tell anyone her name.
You'll understand I'm not to blame.
It's confidential you will see
And musn't be released by me.
My lips are sealed, though you implore
I cannot tell you anymore.
You understand and must agree;
That Liz Weir's secret's safe with me!

Billy Ritchie

The Lesson

Or a bit of a barney in heaven)

Some angels were sitting in paradise west
Engrossed in their sweet angelic things
Like singing their never-ending choral
And strumming their heavenly strings.

When suddenly up from the background
A voice of dissention was heard
"This heavenly music is all very well
But there's other stuff I'd have preferred!"

Gabriel gaped in amazement,
"For ten thousand years and before
It's the only thing we've been playing
Do you mean to tell us there's more?"

"Well of course there is," piped the dissenter
"Of many and various kinds
If you'll whist for a minute I'll tell you,
Provided, that is, you don't mind.

There's pop and there's jazz and there's country
On earth they have made it an art,
Music for singing and dancing
To lighten and gladden the heart."

"And don't forget Irish tradition!"
Butts in Pat , who had lived in Ardoyne,
"I'll give you a couple of verses
And hope that with me you will join."

Then he rendered a couple of ballads,
Some of them short, others long,
But as he got high with excitement
He slipped in the odd party song.

Up shouts Sammy, who'd lived up the Shankill,
"Houl' on!" and tried Pat's voice to quell,
"I'm enjoying the songs and the singer,
But we had traditions as well!"
Then he strummed a few chords on his harp strings
And burst into song right away,
Made his way through "The Sash" and "The Green Grassy Slopes"
And then he blared out "Dolly's Brae".

Pat shouts, "Get a grip of your halo!"
As he gestured his hands in the air
And at once conjured up an oul' fiddle,
(I'm told that they can do that up there).
And he started to play like an expert,
Lively jigs, hornpipes and reels.
The crowd gathered round seemed to like it
And soon they were kicking their heels.

This made Sammy feel he'd been outdone.
Thinks he, "I'll take him down a peg."
Had a go at this conjuring objects
And quickly produced a 'lambeg'
Which he started to batter with gusto
As on earth he had done on "The Twelfth"
Sending out noise and vibrations
Sufficient to bring down the delph.

The sound that he made was tremendous
And the onlookers felt the effect,
There were harps thrown aside, other instruments made
As they tried to get in on the act.
With all of these musical gadgets
It seemed they were forming a band
But as all different tunes they were playing
It very soon got out of hand!

All was just noise and confusion
The songs just a jumble of squalls,
It came out like some fellas from Wicklow
Were trying to guard Derry's walls.
The racket they made was quite awful.
Oul' Nick bellowed up, "Do you mind?
I've a headache," he banged on the ceiling,
"And you lot sound worse than my kind!"

In the midst of it all Pat was fiddlin'
Attempting the 'Wearin' of the Green,'
While Sammy was laceing away at the drum
While trying to render 'The Queen'.
The noise and commotion continued
You never heard worse since you're born.
Gabriel's face was a picture
As he tried to tune in with his horn,

But seeing that this was quite useless
He gave it one almighty blast.
The note nearly shattered their eardrums
But brought on a silence at last.
"Now look here!" he starts up somewhat sternly
"This bedlam leaves me at a loss,
But I'm only a sort of a gaffer,
We'd best hear the word of the boss."

So they mentally tuned in the stillness
And each heard, like a voice, in his head.
"Music and jollification are fine,
But discord is useless" it said.
"Now I know some of you are newcomers,
And I'm all for singing and mirth,
But some of you still have a little to learn,
That you should have done while on the earth.

In your time there I strove, via conscience
As daily I tried to get through
But you seemed to prefer gross material things
Instead of a spiritual view.
But I am reality, sure as the wind,
Though like it, you don't actually see,
Take all living things in the universe wide
And the sum total constitutes ME.
Thus without one I cannot be complete
And in fulness I haven't a name,
Though some call me Nature while others say God,
Use what you will, I'm the same.
I can not be confined to a "Man on a Throne",
For I am Life, wide and sublime.
I cover the limitless reaches of space
And stretch over aeons of time.
But how can you hope for at-one-ment with me,
That something you can't really see
If you can't harmonise with yourselves gathered here
And I find that you all disagree?
On earth as you were, so now you must be
As your subconscious records you haul
The truth from yourself you can't hide or escape,
But progress is open to all,
Continue on efforts if you would reside
On the plains of the eternal day
Travelling to realms of ecstatic joy
And harmony's surely the way."
At that the voice faded and all gathered there
Looked sheepishly round at the rest.
The message was patent the discord must cease,
They knew it was all for the best.
I can tell you this story is truthful,
On that point I nearly would swear,
For I got the whole tale at a seance
From one of the lads who was there.
And since that time all have been happy,
None of them ever looked back,
And they'll say, when our time comes to join them,
"Leave your coat and come in for the crack!"

Billy Ritchie

19

The Orange "Pilgrims"

The pilgrimage coach came to lift us,
To take us away down to Thurles,
And big Mary Rose from the Springfield
Was proud of her hair set in curls.

We crowded round, some clutching liquor
Especially brought for the trip,
With most bottles already sampled
By considerably more than a sip.

In the midst of us there were two strangers
Whom no one had seen there before
And nobody asked for their tickets
As we all scrambled in through the door.

They just seemed to flop on the back seat
And soon the coach got underway
But we gathered, although they were tipsy,
That their first names were Lily and May.

They just sat and tippled their whiskey,
And to tell you the truth, so did I.
By the time we were crossing the border
A few of the travellers were high.

Then some of us started off singing,
Though Lily and May didn't join,
But they let out a gulder, "Up Billy!"
Just as we crossed over the Boyne.

Soon after we pulled in at Dublin,
A break prearranged to have lunch,
Where Lily and May staggered gaily
And got off with the rest of the bunch.

We straightened up as we assembled,
Though Lil and May cared not the least
And they weren't even slightly embarrassed
When they came face to face with a priest!

Lil says, "Hi! Listen here fella,
'Til I put a word in your ear.
I think you'd be better to scarper,
I doubt if you'll be welcome here!"

The wee priest says, "Pardon me madam,
On your state I don't wish to encroach,
But surely you ought to be sober
Since you're just off a pilgrimage coach."

"Pilgrimage? What?" exclaims Lily,
As a good look around her she made,
"This morning we set off for Bangor,
To go to an orange parade."

Well, hearing amidst the confusion,
"What's all this?" questions big Mary Rose,
Still under effects of the liquor,
You could tell by the red of her nose.

"Now calm down," says Father John Reilly,
"The ladies just made a mistake."
"Mistake is it?" bellowed big Rosie,
"She'd be needing a slap on the bake."

"Why you big fenian hussy!" yells Lily,
Making to grab Rosie's throat,
But wee Father John got between them
Which only got on both their goat.

"Well! You oul' orange bitch you," screams Rosie
Ignoring the priest's warning call,
Made a charge and they all lost their balance
And fell into the Royal Canal!

That dampened their urge to do battle
And hastened an end to their war.
Rosie and Lil had to suffer our laughter
While stuck to the oxters in glar.

If looks could have killed I can tell you
They'd have slaughtered the half of the bus,
But the miracle was they stopped fightin'
And directed their venom at us!

We got them fished out and their perfume
Was 'Eau de Canal Bottom Stink'
The saga had not helped appearance
But had countered effects of the drink!

They muttered and cursed as we sniggered
And called them a fine matching pair.
Gone was the make-up from Lily
And the curls had all left Rosie's hair.

A shower, then some lunch and refreshments,
Not to mention a quick change of clothes.
Soon we were ready for leaving.
It was then that a problem arose.

We wanted to make up lost time now,
But what about Lily and May?
We could not leave them stranded in Dublin,
It was best that they came all the way.

Of this they were somewhat reluctant,
But against it they balanced their need,
And not wishing to cause any further delay,
They made a snap choice and agreed.

On arrival at our destination
They came with us, both bold as brass,
Right up to the door of the chapel,
But drew lines at attending the mass.

When back on the coach home to Belfast
Reflecting the chain of events
Rose and Lil thought the whole thing hilarious,
And them from both sides of the fence.

Rosie got great friends with Lily,
And Lily became her best pal,
Though Lil often said, "You're a Baptist
Since that episode in the canal!"

And every time Father John Reilly
Encounters a coach bound for Thurles
He always remembers the day that
He went for a dip with the girls!

Billy Ritchie.

The Dalin' Matchmaker

Both the common and quite unexpected
Take place in affairs of the heart,
Some meet as fate seems to direct it
And some through the matchmaker's art.

Let me tell you of Johnny McCrunkle
As the tale was related to me
Just a stone's throw he lived from me uncle
And led life as a bachelor free.

Such freedom to him was a treasure
A freedom he swore to maintain
He could go and come back at his leisure
Thus single he chose to remain.

Through farming and being quite thrifty
He saved while he lived on his own
Until he was something past fifty
He began to feel much more alone.

It seemed that the farmwork got harder
And the chores round the house seemed to grow
How farm and the kitchen and larder
To handle he just didn't know.

Well, one night he though it all over
As he stared at the bare earthen flure
"I thought that my lifestyle was clover
But now I'm not feeling so sure."

Then he thought about widow McClancy
Who in youth had been one of his aims
In those years past for her he'd a fancy
And old coals easily kindle to flames.

For him she still had an attraction,
The lady was still in her prime.
The years had been kind to complexion
And for her he still had a shine.

He'd a word with fly Freddie the daler,
As down in the bar they'd a sup
As they drank on a deal for a baler,
"Do you think you could get me fixed up?"

Fly Freddie thought fast and he wondered,
How much is there in it for me?
"Are you willing to part with a hundred?
If you are then I'll try and we'll see."

They sealed with a couple of whiskies
And Fred saw the widow that week,
On a pretext of buying some cattle,
To use such excuse he'd the cheek!

In her yard in a casual discussion
With an innocent face, free of blame,
Brought John in without any fussin'
By casually mentioning his name.

His expression was one of no sinner,
Not giving the slightest away,
Though he knew he was on to a winner
When she said, "Come in for some tay."

Over tea as her keeness he measured,
Prompting her with the odd lie,
A thirty year memory she treasured,
He knew by the gleam in her eye!

He spoke and his eyes they were twinkling,
"To live all alone seems absurd
You've a soft spot for John I've an inkling,
Would you like me to put in a word?"

She pretended to stall for a minute,
But admitted she had to agree.
Then Fred broached the subject, "What's in it?
Would there be - say - a hundred, for me?"

"Alright," she replied, "Never fear it,
 There'll be one hundred pounds in your han'
But for God's sake don't let Johnny hear it.
Don't tell him it's part of a plan."

Says Freddie, "My silence is golden,"
And fixed it all up the next day,
Soon two hundred pounds he was foldin'
The affair had took off right away!

The marriage caused minor sensation
And Freddie was there by request
Not sure of by whose invitation
For both had him there as their guest!

In the years since they wed neither wondered
Both stuck to their secrets like glue
Each thinking the dale cost a hundred
Ne'er knowing it really cost two!

Billy Ritchie

The Wooden Leg

There are many from this island who have gone to plains afar
Where they or their descendants would engage
In the field of pioneering or excelling in a war
That forever stamped their name on history's page.

The most of such activities were in America,
And of one called Stonewall Jackson I now tell
His people hailed from Birches in the County of Armagh
He fought the Civil War and fought it well.

His troops he led successfully in skirmish and campaign
Victorious in many battlefields
In struggles of the Civil War he always seemed to gain
And was beaten only once, (by General Shields.)

If ever feeling fearful, well he didn't let it show
And would stand while powder dwindled to a dreg
Now I'll let you in a secret that there's not so many know
That in one such mêlée he lost a leg.

Confined in convalescence it appears his thoughts would roam
With a question pondered o'er, "Perhaps I should?"
Then deciding, sent a letter off to his ancestral home
That he'd like a leg of native Irish wood.

For a while relations argued as to just what they should send
But found an answer they could all agree
From their orchard (it seemed obvious) decided in the end
On a piece of native Armagh apple tree.

From this the leg was fashioned, he delighted to receive
But noticed leaves were sprouting from the start
And each year after that though there's few who do believe
It produced enough to make an apple tart!

Billy Ritchie.

Seamus Lavery

Seamus Lavery lives in Belfast where he works as a school caretaker and writes in his spare time. He is in constant demand as a performer and has had several plays produced. His verse has come to the public's attention following broadcasts on the "Gerry Anderson Show." He has caused the telephone lines in the BBC to become jammed and there have been many requests for his work to be published.

The Cricket

Mrs. Caldwell's little cricket couldn't sing a note,
Because, as she
Discovered, he
Had something in his throat.
She took him to a vet who said,
"Oh dear, without a doubt
This poor wee lad is very bad,
His tonsils must come out.
This operation takes some time
And overnight he'll stay,
But I guarantee
That he will be
Back home within a day,
So leave him here,
With me my dear
And call again tomorrow."
Then off went Mrs. Caldwell
All alone and full of sorrow.
She called next day to fetch him
And flew into a rage,
Because the vet had given her
A canary in a cage.
"I want my cricket back."
She yelled,
While dancing like a fairy,
The vet replied,
"He's there,
Inside,
That greedy wee canary."

Seamus Lavery

My Wee House

It was only a wee house, as wee houses go,
Two rooms upstairs and two down below,
With the dur always open and no thought of danger,
But a warm hearty welcome for friend and for stranger.

Though it was only oil cloth that covered the flur,
It was always kept clean, aye , clean to be sure,
With a big wooden table I'd scrubbed almost white,
And a black-leaded hearth, with fire burning bright.

It was not always tidy and not always neat,
When the childer played games on the flur at m'feet,
But at least they were happy, as happy cud be,
And that was the main thing that mattered to me.

It had no central heating, yet always was warm,
And it kept us all safe through manys a storm,
And on coul winter nights, round the fire we wud sit,
While the childer toul stories, I'd listen and knit.

On Saturday nights, with the wee ones all in,
I'd bring in the big bath, made out of tin,
When I had them all washed, and safely in bed,
I wud sit on the sofa, and shower m'poor head.

I didn't have much, and what I had was soon gone,
But sure if I ran short there was always the pawn,
When the shoes and the clothes that we wore every Sunday,
Were cleaned and wrapped up for me Uncle's on Monday.

Aye, them was the days that they say was hard,
When to go to the toilet, y'went to the yard,
And y'sat w'yer feet lifted aff the flur,
When the rain or the snow blew in under the dur.

Ah but many's the day when the sun wud shine,
We wud go on a tram to the end of the line,
Where I'd sit on m'shawl, and think it was grand,
As m'childer played games on the Greencastle sand.

And on warm summer evenings, I wud git m'wee stool,
And I'd sit at the dur with m'needles and wool,
Sometimes I wud knit and other times darn,
While me and wee Cassie wud have a quare yarn.

Then things started changin', for better or worse,
And some o'them changes t'me was a curse,
For the gas was tuk out, and electric put in,
And the bills I'd t'pay then, was really a sin.

And with T.V.s and such things I was near driv mad,
For m'childer just wanted what all their friends had,
And I knew that t'plase them, I wud always be poor,
For the tick-men were nivir away from m'dur.

Well, the years rolled by, and with m'childer all grown,
And all of them married, w'homes of their own,
I thought I'd have pace, there bein' just him and me,
But oh dear no, this was not to be.

For a lock o'months back, this letter did come,
Which said my wee house was only a slum,
My lovely wee house, that knowed sweet times and bitter,
Was now called a slum, by some City Hall scitter.

Well I nearly dropped dead where I stud on the flur,
When in comes wee Cassie, m'neighbour next dur,
The colour of death, and I wasn't much better,
And she had in her hand, the very same letter.

The rest of m'neighbours had got letters too,
And it seemed there was nothing at all we cud do,
We had protest marches all over the place,
And we argued until we were blue in the face.

But them City Hall ones are a very tough foe,
And the end of it all was, we just had to go,
And the day I was lavin', I lingered a while,
Just to be with the friends I had knowed from a chil'.

When I redd out m'wee house, m'heart was real sore,
And I thought m'house sensed, I'd be back there no more,
For the dur gave a screech, and the windys all shook,
As I stud on the futpath, t'have my last look.

Well, they putt him an' me in a high rise flat,
With people on this side, and people on that,
With people above us and people below,
But not one friendly face in that place did I know.

In my own wee house I cud always luk out,
And see the wee childer all playin' about,
An' take m'wee stool, and sit at the dur,
But in this flat I cud just see the sky and the flur.

Then one day last week I went out for a dander,
And they say where the heart lies, the feet always wander,
I walked to the street where I'd lived all my life,
First as a child and then as a wife.

When I saw my wee house, I just stud there and cried,
I felt coul all over, and empty inside,
My house, that had sheltered my family and me,
Was stripped bare and naked, for all eyes to see.

The hall dur was lyin' down flat on the flur,
And the kitchen was covered with plaster and stur,
The slates were all gone, and the rafters as well,
And my lovely wee house was now just a shell.

Then down the street came this great big crane,
With a big iron ball on a long heavy chain,
It stopped just fernenst me, and then swung round,
And my poor helpless house was brought to the ground.

I opened my mouth, but I just cudn't spake,
And I had the same feelin' y'get at a wake,
A lifetime of caring, had just come to an end,
And I'd just seen the death of a very dear friend.

For my house was a home, a home full of life,
A haven of love, in a world full of strife,
A place of comfort, a refuge from pain,
And now it was gone, with one swing of a crane.

I turned on m'heel, and m'legs were shakin'
I walked slowly away, with a heart that was breakin'
I went towards that flat, with a feelin' of dread,
And I wished, like my wee house, I wished I was dead.

Seamus Lavery

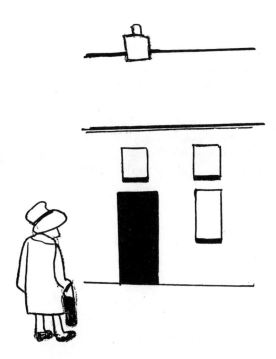

Sisters

There was a young lassie lived over the hill,
She never got wed and it seemed never will;
And her fate was the topic all over the place,
Because she'd been born with a very plain face.

She had a young sister, a beauty so rare
That women and menfolk would just stand and stare,
And wonder why nature could be such a twister,
To give such a beauty, a plain ugly sister.

And even at dances boys deemed it their duty,
To dance all night long with this fair raving beauty,
Whilst there in the corner, left all on her own
Sat the poor ugly sister, forlorn and alone.

But fate has a strange way of turning things round,
And the poor ugly sister, a husband she found.
And the things people said then were really unkind
For the husband, though handsome, was totally blind.

And when people spoke of his wife's ugly features,
He'd smile and he'd pity those talkative creatures,
Because visible beauty with age must depart,
While true love and beauty lives deep in the heart.

There's an old winkled woman lives over the hill,
She never got wed and it seems never will,
For the youth and the beauty that once was her own,
She squandered and wasted, and now lives alone.

Seamus Lavery

My Friend Jack

A friend is one who grieves when we are sad,
A friend is one who smiles when we are glad.
When fear or anger tend to blur our sight,
A friend will always try to keep us right.

And though our friend has problems just like us,
He smiles and tries to solve them without fuss.
If everything around us seems to fall,
Our friend will strive to keep us walking tall.

And when we are right our friend will tell us so;
If we are wrong, he'll quietly let us know,
And if to us the world's a dreary place,
Our friend will put a smile back on its face.

The day will come, they say, when friends must part,
But friendship that is rooted in the heart
Remains forever, radiant and sublime,
And is unchanged by distance or by time.

Seamus Lavery

The Weeping Tree

I am a tree, I cannot move, I cannot run away,
My roots are firmly in the ground and here for life I stay.
The One who put me here knows best, I'm part of His great plan,
To make the world a better place, for birds, for beast and man.

Amongst my branches, strong and firm, young birds can make their
    nest,
Whilst man, from rain and scorching sun within my shade shall rest.
The berries and the fruit I bear to all I freely give,
So man and beast can have a feast and free from want may live,

Oil and coal I have produced for mankinds' every need,
Yet men forever wanting more, through selfishness and greed,
Their appetites to satisfy, their cravings to fulfil,
Made bows and arrows, clubs and spears, their fellow man to kill.

Helpless here I stand and weep and fear that dreadful day,
When men shall come with ripping saws to cut my life away,
No fruit nor berries shall I bear, no place for birds to nest,
For I'm a silly stupid tree and wise men know what's best.

Yet I was here for quite some time before man walked this earth.
I saw the coming of the birds, I witnessed man's first birth,
And I recall that awful day when man cut down a tree,
To crucify to death the One Who made both man and me.

Seamus Lavery

The Old Lamp Post

All day long, he'd stand and wait
On the footpath, by the old school gate.
His arms outstretched, his head held high,
A friendly twinkle in his eye.
And when he'd hear the school bell ring,
His happy heart would start to sing.
For he knew that soon, without a doubt
The children would come tumbling out
And scrambling with impatient haste
They'd tie their ropes around his waist
And how he loved to hear them sing
As round and round and round they'd swing.
For many years this had been so
As he watched the little children grow
And when they were too big to swing
Their own little children they would bring.
And even on an Autumn night
He'd lure them with his friendly light,
While at his feet they'd sit and tell
Of ghosts and witches and devils from Hell.
And when the children went home to sleep
A lonely vigil he would keep
And all night long his heart would ache
As he waited for the dawn to break.
This was the life he had always known,
Pleasing children he called his own,
Watching them grow, then fade away
While other children came to play.
This was his world, this little street
With happy children around his feet
To please them was his life's endeavour
And here he would remain forever.

But dawned a day of rain and sleet
When men came digging around his feet
And he wondered why in the stinging rain
That around his waist they had tied a chain
And as that chain began to grip
He felt his feet slither and slip
And the earth beneath began to quake
And his body began to sway and shake.
And the scream he gave made not a sound
As he glimpsed the fast approaching ground.
Oh! There he lay, bewildered and sore
For he knew he would stand on his feet no more.
No more he'd hear the school bell ring,
No more he'd hear his children sing.
Again in panic he tried to shout
As the fading light in his eye went out.
Then his body was gripped with a frightening chill,
He rolled on his side, then lay - quite still

The school bell rang with a mournful sound,
The old lamp's children gathered around.
They stood and stared at an empty space
While tears streamed down each little face.
In every hand was a dangling rope
But each tiny heart was void of hope
And a sobbing voice was heard to say
"Oh! Why did they take our lamp away?"

Seamus Lavery

Una

When all the world
Seems full of hatred,
Cold, and unforgiving,
The simple love
Of one pure heart,
Shall still make life
Worth living.

When tight clenched fists
In anger rise,
When hurtful words
Are spoken,
The silent love
In a baby's eyes,
Can soothe the heart that's broken.

Seamus Lavery

The Daisy and the Dandelion

The daisy and the dandelion
   Growing side by side,
Listened to the buttercup,
   Glowing with self pride.
"All the little children love me,"
   He was heard to mutter,
"They hold me underneath their chins,
   And ask if they like butter."

The dainty little daisy smiled,
   Then said with an impish wink.
"What you have said is very true,
   Though should you pause and think,
When next you're held beneath a chin,
   You've no cause to be vain,
For around the neck of the little child,
   You'll find a daisy chain."

'Twas then the dandelion spoke,
   With words both soft and slow,
"The names I'm called are hurtful,"
   And his voice was sad and low,
"But later on, when my flower is gone,
And my head is old and grey,
   The children shall caress me then,
When I tell the time of day."

Seamus Lavery

My Mother's Shawl

The sky was dark and when prayers were said,
My mother happed us up in bed,
My father was working across the sea,
And we'd prayed to God that safe he'd be.

The sky was red and sparks were flying,
When I woke to the sound of my mother crying,
My brothers and sisters were crying as well,
And I thought I had wakened up somewhere in Hell.

There were loud banging noises all over the place,
And the red burning sky shone on everyone's face,
People were screaming and yelling outside
And along with my brothers and sisters, I cried.

The floor of the bedroom was glistening red,
Where reflecting splinters of glass lay spread,
My mother 'tween crying and saying her prayers,
Led us to safety, under the stairs.

With her shawl wrapped around us, she held us close to her,
And I felt fear and strong love go trembling through her,
With each loud explosion, she drew us all tight,
And prayed, "Sacred Heart, please protect us this night."

We sat in the darkness, weeping and groaning,
My mother's arms round us, rocking and moaning,
And the hot burning tears she shed with each moan,
Fell on our cheeks and were mixed with our own.

Then one loud explosion drowned all other sound,
Shook all the walls and trembled the ground,
And in that loud silence, I knew I was dreaming,
As it seemed from a distance, my mother was screaming.

She hurried us out as the house kept shaking,
And under my bare feet, I felt the floor quaking,
She opened the hall door and there she did stand,
Pleading for someone to give her a hand.

We all stood behind her, gripping her skirt,
Shivering with fear and covered with dirt,
But oh, how I wished she would close the hall door,
And return to the darkness and safety once more.

For the scene in that street where I loved to play,
Is etched in my memory 'til my dying day,
A cauldron of strangers were swirling around,
Where planks, bricks and slates lay all over the ground.

Sharp piercing whistles rained down through the air,
As the people crouched low with a loud wailing prayer,
And every explosion brought forth a hot gust,
Of black blinding smoke and dry choking dust.

A deep throbbing noise from the sky overhead,
Filled me with wonder, with fear, and with dread,
And it seemed that this mad world, while passing us by,
Had turned a deaf ear to my poor mother's cry.

Despairing of help, she closed the hall door,
And guided us back to the coal-hole once more,
Where all that long night, which seemed like a year,
We sat 'til she whimpered, "Thank God... the all-clear."

With her shawl still around us, she sighed with relief,
And the tears that she shed now were not tears of grief,
She hugged us, she kissed us, she wept with delight,
And thanked God for helping her all through that night.

Then out to the kitchen we scrambled once more,
Where the ceiling and black soot covered the floor,
We washed and got dressed as best as we could,
And went round to the school for hot tea and food.

On my way to the school I got quite a fright,
At the place where I'd played that previous night,
Where a woman had chased us away from her door,
There was now only rubble... there were houses no more.

Later that day, amidst panic and fuss,
With clothes tied in bundles, we boarded a bus,
Where we all sat in silence, bewildered and dazed,
And passed along streets where houses still blazed.

The streets became roads I had ne'r before seen,
Flanked by hedges and square fields of green,
We were brought to a farmhouse as a new night was falling,
And I listened in awe to different birds calling.

Weary and tired we went in through the door,
And stood on a big broad flag-stoned floor.
In amazement I gazed at a fire by the wall,
That had neither fender, nor grating at all.

From the ceiling two oil lamps gave off a soft light,
And the scene was so peaceful it put fear to flight,
With the sweet scent of turf smoke I'd not smelt before,
I closed my eyes slowly and saw nothing more.

Well, we stayed in the country for almost a year,
Away from the bombs and free from all fear,
Where I learned to make butter and helped to make hay,
And discovered new things about life every day.

One time coming home from school through the fields,
I noticed a hen with her chicks at her heels,
She saw me and spread out her wings like a hood,
Then wrapped them around her poor frightened brood.

No author can write, nor orator speak,
Of the love mothers have for the young and the weak,
As I looked at that hen, I could nought but recall,
That night I had sheltered 'neath my mother's shawl.

Seamus Lavery

Bill Nesbitt

Bill Nesbitt lives in County Antrim but his fame as a writer of verse has spread far and wide through publication in a weekly column in "The Sunday World" and through many broadcasts.

Bill is modest about his work, describing himself as "just an oul' cod of a rhymer," but he has a wonderful knack of capturing the local scene, warts and all, and forcing people to take a long hard look at themselves. "The Angel of Sandy Row" is probably his best known piece. It is often requested at public storytelling events and has been performed on Ulster Television by Billy Ritchie, another of the writers in this book.

The Angel of Sandy Row

One Saturday night, I'd been having a jar
And was walking back home from a Sandy Row bar -
I'd had far too many, it wasn't a joke,
So I turned up an entry to have a good boke...
When I lifted my head, I began to feel sicker,
And swore, there and then, that I'd give up the liquor,
For, standing before me, all shiny and bright,
Was a figure that gave me one helluva fright...
He'd great, flowing robes that came down to his ankle -
The likes of him never was seen up the Shankill!
Sez he, "I'm an angel!"... sez I, "You're a what?"
Sez he, "I'm an angel!"... sez I, "That you're not -
If you're really an angel, then where are your wings,
And why aren't you plucking your heavenly strings,
And surely you've got better places to go
Than standing up entries in old Sandy Row?"
Sez he, "Willie, dear, I'm here in disguise,
For I'm one of the Old Boy's heavenly spies
(Though, up there, they think I'm a bit of a laugh,
For my number is double-oh-six and a half!)
He's sent me to Ulster to look at the scene,
And to find out the difference 'twixt Orange and Green,
For we've heard nasty rumours that Satan is grinning,
And that evil and badness in Ulster are winning...!"
Sez I, "Mister, dear, it's the truth that you're speaking,
For the Fenians all over the Province are sneaking -
They're getting in everywhere, Lord, but they're tricky...
You couldn't be up to the games of a Mickey!"
Well, the angel he looked at me hard, for a while,
Then he lifted his head, and he gave a wee smile -
It was like he was laughing at some private joke,
And a feeling of anger in me was awoke.
So I sez, "Listen, Mac - are you Fenian or Prod?"
Sez he, "Willie, dear, I'm the same as my God,
And He doesn't care if you're black, or your white,
If you're Orange or Green, or you're left, or you're right,

If you're family's all Prods, or Fenians, or Yids,
For everyone here is just one of His kids..."
Now, you'll agree that a statement like that was a shocker -
It was clear as a bell he was clean off his rocker...
And he surely knew nothing at all about God
If he thought that a Mick was as good as a Prod!
Was he out on his geg? Was he having a jest?
I decided to put the idea to the test,
So, sez I, "Tell us this - have you heard of King Billy?
Or even the Sash, or the fair Orange Lily?
Do you know of the Blues, or of brave Derry's walls?
Did you know that Old Nick has a house on the Falls?"
Well, he just shook his head, and leaned back on the wall,
So, sez I, "Do you not know your Bible at all?"
Now, I go to my church, like a decent Prod should,
And decided to do the poor fellow some good,
And I said, "Tell you what - I'm taking you home,
And, before you go back, you'll know all about Rome -
When you're up there in Heaven, you'll have lots new to tell...
Like, for instance, the divil speaks Gaelic in Hell!"
Well, in no time at all, we were back at my house,
And there, at the door, was Big Jinny, my spouse,
And the look on her face made me weak at the knees,
So, quick as a flash, sez I, "Jinny, please,
I want you to meet a good buddy of mine -
I don't know his name, but his number'll do fine...
He's one of those spies, like that double-oh-seven...
And, believe it or not, his headquarters is heaven...
He's come for his supper, so get out the pan
And give him a feed that is fit for a man!'
Well, her face was a picture, but, give her due,
She stuck out her hand, and said "How d'you do?
From Heaven to Belfast is many a mile,
So, now that you're here, you must stop for a while!'
One thing about Jinny, she knows how to bake,
And there, on the table she put... ANGEL cake!
Your man was quite pleased (you could tell by his face),
And he said, "Here, I'm glad I came down to this place!'
Well, after the teas we sat down for a chat,

And we talked about this and we talked about that,
And I told him the way things were in Belfast,
And how all the Prods would fight to the last
To maintain our religion the best that we could
The way that our forefathers said that we should,
I told him about my own L.O.L.,
And I showed him my sash (and I wore it as well),
And then I brought out my wee Orange flute
And decided to give it a bit of a toot...
I played him "The Sash", and I played "Dolly's Brae"...
Sez he, "Willie, dear, you fairly can play -
But lend me your flute, and I'll give you an air
That's just a bit different from those you played there!"
So I gave him the flute, and he started to play...
Lord, I'll never forget it till my dying day,
For the notes that he played made us sit there, quite still -
They rose up in the air, the whole house to fill...
They were soft, they were sweet... they brought tears to my eyes...
And I suddenly felt... so old and so wise...
Then a funny thing happened... I tell you no lie...
Your man touched my arm - and I started to FLY...
With him at my side, I rose in the air,
And out of the house, over Shaftesbury Square -
I was so bloomin' scared that I started to shiver,
And my arms and my legs were all of a quiver
As the two of us kept floating on through the night,
Passing the old City Hall on the right,
And there was the shipyard, the Dufferin Dock,
The Liverpool boat, and the grand Albert Clock,
And there were the people, the girls and the boys,
And the lights of the city, the smell and the noise,
The hooting of horns... and also, of course,
The police and the army were down there in force -
We stepped up the pace, and began to fly faster...
Lord, meeting your man was a downright disaster!
We soared up the Falls, towards Andersonstown...
And that's where we stopped... I had a look down...
The rooves of the houses were sort of transparent -
The reason, to me, was not too apparent,

But one little house I especially spied...
I could see right into the bedroom inside -
You could tell, at a glance, where THEIR loyalties lay,
For the Pope on the wall gave their leanings away!
And there was a man, on a wee wicker chair,
With a frown on his face, and a sad hopeless stare..
And a woman was there at the foot of the bed...
When I looked further up my heart turned to lead -
When I saw what was there, I just couldn't help crying,
For there, on that bed, a youngster lay, dying -
And the funny thing was, when I saw it was sick,
It just didn't matter that it was a Mick...
Those Fenians might breed families of nine,
But that child could easily have been one of mine,
And its father could easily have been my own brother -
Sure, the Prods and the Micks were just like each other...
Now, whether or not, 'twas because of the drink,
For the first time in ages, I started to think,
And I found I was telling myself to act wise,
And to look all around me, and open my eyes...
Now, all of the time I was watching that room,
His nibs on the flute was still playing that tune -
He handled the instrument just like a master...
Then, all of a sudden the tempo got faster
And we started to move away from Belfast,
Away from the present, and back to the past...
The music, it brought me right back to my youth,
To the first girl I loved, my darling wee Ruth...
I could see her again, her eyes, and her smile...
I could see us again, at the wee country stile...
And remembered the way that our families turned odd,
For she was a Mick... and I was a Prod...
I saw it again, the night Ruthie died,
And the way that her family kept me outside...
I remembered all this, and felt so... so sad,
For MY folks turned out to be just as bad -
They told me to marry into my own,
Instead of a girl whose allegiance was Rome -
And, remembering this, I knew very well

There were Prods as well as Mickies in Hell!
I remembered, as well, that God sent His Son
To say "Love Your Neighbour" and he meant EVERY one...
And while I remembered, the music played on...
Then it stopped... I looked up... the angel was... gone...
Well, the next thing I knew, I woke up in my bed
With a mouth like a sewer, and a bomb in my head,
And Jinny was lying there, tonguing and screaming...
Everything normal! I must have been dreaming!
But that dream was a dream that filled me with shame,
And, from that day to this, I've not been the same,
For the music I heard lingers on in my mind,
And I swear that I'll never again be so blind -
Till the day that I die, I'll treat all men the same...
Even the ones with a Catholic name!
And, if God thinks I'm worth it, He'll take me to Heaven
And make me a spy... maybe double-oh-seven?
And then, perhaps, some day, if you're up Sandy Row,
And up a wee entry you might have to go,
Who knows? You might see me, in a shiny white suit,
And there, in my hand, my wee Orange flute...
And, if you ask me, real nice, I might play you that tune...
But, for now, I'm away... sure, I'll see you... real soon...

Bill Nesbitt

The Return of the Angel

There's a tale that I've told, how a long time ago,
I encountered an angel in old Sandy Row.
Well, you mightn't believe it, but let me explain,
Last Saturday night I met him again!
I've got to confess, I'd been out on the tear,
For that woman of mine had got in my hair.
Sure, you know when these women are going to town
You need an odd jar to help you cool down,
And you'll maybe, at times swallow more than you should,
And find it's not doing a ha'p'orth of good?
Well, that's how I felt, just as bad as could be,
Not helped by the fact that I'd eaten no tea.
I decided I'd better head home to my bed,
For my poor head was spinning, my feet were like lead,
And I hadn't the strength left to finish my jar,
When, suddenly, someone walked up to the bar.
When I saw who it was, I near fell on my face,
For not many angels come into that place!
It was him, sure enough, right there in MY pub,
As long as I lived, I'd remember HIS gub
(Although he was wearing a sort of disguise,
With the peak of his duncher pulled over his eyes.)
Says he, "It's yerself! Well, give us yer han',
It's manys a minute I've minded ye, man!
Come on and sit down on thon chairs at the back,
And we'll have a wee jar, and a bit of a crack!"
Says I, "Thank ye kindly, and mine's is a Coke,
For if I have any more, I'm going to boke.
I've had far to many, another will kill me,
So a wee glass of Coke will just about fill me."
Says he, "I don't know what ye're worried about,
For what good's an angel, if he cannot help out?"
And he stretched out his hand and he put it on mine,
And would you believe it, I began to feel fine.
Says I, "Now ye're talkin', and mine's is a stout,

And maybe ye'll tell me just what ye're about,
And just why ye're here in a Sandy Row bar,
For, surely YOUR lot are forbidden to jar?"
Says he, "Willie, dear, I've got dispensation,
For Ulster's a very peculiar nation,
And, when we're assigned to a duty down here,
We're permitted to have the occasional beer,
For it's hard on the nerves here, ye're bound till agree,
And there's nobody, Willie, more nervous than me!"
So yer man, he goes up, and, says he, "It's my shout,"
And comes back with two half-uns, and two pints of stout,
And then we sat down, and we talked of Belfast,
And the way things had been since he visited last,
The troubles, the heartaches, the sorrows, the joys,
Then a voice from behind us said, "Pardon me boys.
D'ye mind if I join yez, and buy yez a beer,
For I'm all on me own, I'm a stranger round here!"
Well the angel turned round, and went white as a sheet,
And I swear that he nearly fell off of his seat,
As he croaked, with an effort, "Good heavens, it's you!"
And the stranger, he cackled, "Great Hades, that's true!"
Then the angel said, "Willie, I'm feeling fierce sick,
This isn't a stranger, he's a spy, for Oul' Nick!"
The stranger's red eyes gave a smouldering glare,
And brimstone and sulphur pervaded the air
As he turned, and he stared at me, full in the face;
"I'll give ye fair warnin', get out of this place!
This eejit and me have got things till discuss,
And the business we have is just between us!"
Well, I must have been mad (put it down to the drink),
For I started to speak, without stoppin' till think.
Says I, "Listen, Mac, ye're maybe a demon,
But I'm not concerned with whatever ye're schemin'.
For years I've come here for me bottle of stout,
And the divil himself's not for puttin' me out!"
The demon's face blackened, his eyes went on fire,
And I thought for a cert, I was bound till expire.
I began till regret all the things that I'd said,
I'd a feeling I'd soon be quite drastically dead!

He lifted his hands! Lord, I knew I was gone!
Then the angel, says he till the demon, "Houl' on!
Sure, he's just a mere mortal, a pitiful fella,
But you, you're a demon, and I reckon ye're yella
If you use all the powers you have at your whim
To demolish a harmless wee cratur like him!"
"Yella? Who's yella? Not me!", yelled the demon,
Shakin' and stampin' and rantin' and screamin',
"C'mon out the back, and I'll soon sort ye out,
And I'll show ye what bein' a demon's about!"
"Ye're on!" said the angel, his face flamin' red -
Sure it looked like the porter had gone to his head!
I'll show ye, us angels are made of strong stuff.
Ye'll soon change yer tune when ye're cryin' "Enough!"
Well, the two of them ups, and goes out to the entry,
Leaving me there at the door, doing sentry,
And they went round the corner, where I couldn't see,
But the noise of the fight was as loud as could be,
With flashes of lightening, and billows of smoke,
And hailstones, and earthquakes, it wasn't no joke!
I was all of a-tremble, afeared for my life,
Even more feared than I was of the wife!
Then, all of a sudden, it quietened down,
The hush was that deathly, I started to frown,
So still, and so silent, it really was wierd,
And then round the corner the angel appeared!
His nose was all bloodied, he looked awful rough.
I tell you, that punch up, it must have been tough!
Says he, "That'll larn him who's really the boss,
And I think that I've got me wee message across!
He's sittin' there, quiet, and meek as a lamb,
As much of an angel, perhaps as I am!"

Says I, "Well I'm jiggered, for I've always thought
That angels were peaceful, or so I've been taught,
And, somehow, you know, it just doesn't seem right
That an angel should get himself mixed in a fight.
Hard men in heaven? Well I never knew it,
So tell us, oul han', just how did ye do it?"
Said he, "I just taught him some brotherly love,
With the help of a paving stone stuck in me glove,
For devils and demons are hard till persuade,
And I had to use methods like theirs, I'm afraid!
Well, now I must go, and clean myself up,
And I haven't got time, now, to stay for a sup,
But, maybe, some day, you might see me back,
And we'll have that wee jar, and that bit of crack."
Then, would you believe it, I'm telling no lies,
Yer man, he just vanished, in front of my eyes!

    *   *   *   *   *   *   *

Then all of a sudden, I felt my arm taken,
And someone was maulin' me, pullin' and shakin',
And a voice in my ear going yackety-yack,
And there I was, lying in bed on my back.
The missus was nagging away in my ear.
Och, my night on the town was costing me dear,
For my head was a-throbbing, my mouth was all stale,
Had I been dreaming, or had it been real?
But one thing is certain, and one thing is clear,
The divil has surely caused mischief down here,
And Ulster, poor Ulster, is sufferin' sad,
And I'm sure you'll agree that it wouldn't be bad
If someone COULD teach him some brotherly love,
With the help of a pavin'-stone stuck in the glove!

Bill Nesbitt

The Taxi

I met a girl at the village hop, she said her name was Nancy.
She really was a smasher, and to her I took a fancy,
I asked her could I take her home, she said that she was willin' ,
But I had to get a taxi, and it cost me thirty shillin'.

Now, that's a lot of money, so I asked her for the half,
And, boys, but she was stingy, for she turned, and just walked aff.
I had to pay it all meself, it simply wasnae fair,
And surely it was only right that she should pay her share?

Women! Ach, they're all the same, as selfish as can be,
Preyin' on poor eejits, the likes of you and me,
They'd take your last make, so they would, given half the chance,
And take the sting away from it by callin' it 'romance'!

Well, anyway, this Nancy had gone off and left me stranded.
You must admit, her actions were mighty heavy handed,
For that thirty bob was all I had, and och, it made me sick
When the rotten taxi driver wouldnae take me home on tick!

And then the rain came peltin' down, a terrible oul' night,
And I got soaked from head to foot, I must have been a sight.
I walked, and tried to thumb a lift, but nobody would stop,
I tell you, I was scunnered at that stupid village hop!

A good three hours it took me, till I was home in bed,
And, och, the thoughts of vengeance that went runnin' through my
    head!
But, in spite of all the walkin', I found it hard to sleep,
When I thought about that thirty bob, I felt that I could weep!

Well, I saw her at the village hop, time and time again.
A right flirtatious creature, that was brave and plain,
For every week she'd flash her eyes at Tom, or Dick, or Maxie,
And one of them would take her home, and always in a taxi!

Well, I let a wheen of months go by, and then I chanced me arm,
And asked to take her home again, with every ounce of charm,
I acted like the memory of that night was far behind me,
And as far as Nancy was concerned, she really couldn't mind me!

Well, we went home in a taxi, for that was Nancy's style,
And it cost me thirty bob again, but I paid up with a smile,
For I'd found that Nancy's father was the man who did the drivin' -
Because of her, his business was absolutely thrivin'!

So I set me cap at Nancy, and her and me got wed.
I'd always sworn to wed a lass who'd got a business head!
And now we've got three daughters, they're beautiful, and sweet,
And I don't own a taxi, I own a bloomin' fleet!

Bill Nesbitt

Youth

My blood's been thinned
By rain and wind,
My thatch is white as snow,
My body's weak,
My joints a-creak,
I'm getting very slow...
I'm at the stage
Of middle age
(Or somewhat past the middle) -
I'm not one whit
As nearly fit
As that proverbial fiddle…

No longer young,
My spring is sprung,
My strength is disappearing
I've lost my vim,
My edge is dim -
I'm growing hard of hearing…
I have no brawn,
My go has gone,
I'm quite devoid of vigour -
And I'm ashamed
To find I'm framed
In such a fulsome figure!

But every page
Of passing age
Bears witness to a story -
A tale of life
Of pain and strife
Of infamy and glory…
Each line in place
Upon my face
A record of life's rambles -
Of young romance,
And ungrasped chance,
And unrewarded gambles…

A baby's skin,
Unscarred by sin,
By living yet untainted
Is chaste and sweet -
An unused sheet,
A canvas yet unpainted…
But time goes by
And seasons fly
And virtue is diminished,
And years unfold,
And men grow old -
The portrait soon is finished.

To tell the truth,
The thought of youth
Is one that tends to bore me
Nor do I miss
Those days of bliss
When time stretched out before me…
I do not grieve
The boy naive
Remiss in worldly knowledge,
Secure, unfraught,
As yet untaught
The lessons of life's college…

I do not find
My state of mind
The slightest bit depressing…
This vale of tears,
Its woes and fears,
Is something of a blessing…
To sing the praise
Of salad days
Is but a vain endeavour,
For mortal man
Must live his span
And can't stay young forever!

And so, you see,
I'm glad to be
Mature, and ripe, and mellow
With hollowed cheek
And bones that creek
And skin that's turning yellow -
I'd hate the pain
Of youth again,
Its trauma and emotion…
And, should I sigh
For days gone by -
I soon go off the notion…!

Bill Nesbitt

Valentine

My love, it saddens me to say
That Valentine has had his day,
And, though it might seem very hard,
This year, I'm sending you no card.

You're wonderful, oh, lover mine -
The archetype of the Lord's design…
When he created you, I'd say
He threw that perfect mould away…

There's no-one in the world like you,
And that is your opinion, too -
Never one to hide your light,
You're Number One …in your own sight…

You know that you're a raven beauty,
A cuddlesome and comely cutie,
The most alluring man could find
In all the realm of womankind…

Your mirror is your constant friend -
You watch it daily, without end,
Deep in love with your reflection,
Drinking in your own perfection….

You touch your skin, you stroke your hair,
You find yourself exceeding fair,
And smile with pleasure when you feel
The magic of your own appeal…

By yourself, you've been encaptured,
Titillated and enraptured -
The fount of all your inspiration
Lying in self admiration…

You're fascinated and enchanted
By the looks that God has granted -
Quite enamoured with each feature
Of yourself, you lovely creature...

You're everything you've ever dreamed -
You're absolutely self-esteemed -
If you had not been born as you,
I'm sure you would have wanted to!

You find it not the slightest odd
That God has made you so unflawed,
And quite convinced, it seems to me,
You're everything a girl should be...

But all your silly self-adoring
Is beginning to get boring...
If you're so grand, and mighty fine -
Then be your own darned Valentine...!

Bill Nesbitt

Uncle Zebedee

Uncle Zebedee is... dead...
Took a pain inside his head -
Oh, lackaday, and woe is me...
How I miss old Zebedee!

Uncle Zebedee's... defunct...
His spirit, it has upped and bunked...
His body's underneath the clay -
And Lord knows where he is today!

Uncle Zebedee's deceased...
The worms have had a lovely feast...
His old remains have not been wasted -
Wonder how his torso tasted?

Uncle Zebedee's... expired...
From this weary world retired,
Disappeared from human view,
Headed on to pastures new...

Uncle Zebedee is... late...
He's either at the Pearly Gate
Or, much more likely, (as you know),
He's frying in the flames below!

Uncle Zebedee is... snuffed...
Pity we can't have him stuffed,
Preserved in all his pristine glory...
But that would be a little gory...

Uncle Zebedee has... perished...
But his memory is cherished,
And, though his carcass may be rotten,
Zebedee won't be forgotten...

Uncle Zebedee's... concluded...
(Unless, of course, I'm quite deluded -
But, very hopefully, I'm not,
For that would spoil this rhyming plot)...

Uncle Zebedee has... popped...
Entirely and completely stopped -
A most unpleasant way to be...
A shame about old Zebedee!

Uncle Zebedee's... kaput...
Mortified from head to foot,
Drained of all his vital juice,
Lying there, of no more use...

Uncle Zebedee is... lifeless...
Luckily, the man was wifeless -
Had the foresight not to leave
A family behind to grieve...

Uncle Zebedee's... departed...
Everyone is broken-hearted...
His outlook's grim, his future's black,
For Zebedee will not be back...

Uncle Zebedee's... blown out...
Of that, there's not the slightest doubt...
Finished... over... ended... spent...
What a foul predicament!

Uncle Zebedee has... gone...
A sober thought to dwell upon...
That what's occurred to Zebedee
Will come to pass to you and me!

Bill Nesbitt

The Rivals

Whenever I visit a friendly bar
To sample the local ales,
The things I hear
With my eager ear
Inspire my poetic tales.
Many a yarn I've listened to
That's given me great delight,
But none compared
To the one I heard
Down at the pub, last night.

The man on the stool beside me looked
Just a little the worse for wear,
As he turned to me,
"My friend," said he,
"I've a story I'd like to share.
You're a man with a kindly sort of face,
And I know I've got a cheek,
But my burning need
Is great indeed,
And I've simply got to speak!

"You see before you a tortured man,
A being in dark distress,
I've lived for years
In a vale of tears
And deep unhappiness,
And it's all because of a girl I loved,
The fairest in all the land.
Her heart I sought
But a rival fought
For the right to the lady's hand.

"She said that she loved us both the same,
And was torn between the two,
That she couldn't decide
Whose blushing bride
She'd be, or what to do.
And so it was left to the two of us
To sort the thing out right.
And we did, you know,
In a toe-to-toe,
A bloody and bruising fight.

"And that's the reason you see me now,
A man with a broken heart,
A man with an air
Of dark despair,
Whose life has been torn apart."
I said to the man, "I understand.
When love, your life has crossed,
The scars don't heal,
I know how you feel,
And I'm sorry to hear you lost."

He looked at me then with tear stained cheeks,
"It's hard to explain, I guess.
Since that far off night,
When I fought that fight,
I've known great bitterness.
I'm paying the price for my fine romance
And everything I've done,
For that nagging wife
Is the bane of my life.
I didn't lose. I won!"

Bill Nesbitt

The Only Place For Me

I'll speak to you of Belfast, stranger, if you want to know,
So listen, and I'll tell you why I love this city so.

BELFAST... is an Ulsterman, with features dour and grim,
It's a pint of creamy porter, it's a Sunday morning hymn,
A steaming pasty supper, or vinegar with peas,
A homely little cafe where they serve you farmhouse teas,
A banner on July the Twelfth, a sticky toffee apple,
A righteous little Gospel Hall, a Roman Catholic chapel,
A "Tele' boy with dirty face, a slice of apple tart,
A fry upon a Saturday, hot coal brick, on a cart,
A Corporation gas-man, complete with bowler hat,
A wee shop on a corner with a friendly bit of chat,
An old man in a duncher, a woman in a shawl,
A pinch of snuff, a tatie farl, a loyal Orange Hall,
A tobacco smell in York Street, a bag of yellow man,
An Easter egg what's dyed in whin, a slice of Ormo pan,
A youngster with some sprickly-begs inside a wee jam-jar,
A meeting at the Customs House, an old Victorian bar,
Mud banks on the Lagan when the tide is running low,
A man collecting "refuse", bonfires in Sandy Row,
A bag of salty dullis, a bowl of Irish stew,
Goldfish down in Gresham Street, a preacher in a queue,
A portrait of King Billy upon a gable wall,
A flower seller on a stool outside the City Hall,
A half moon round a doorstep, a "polisman" on guard,
A pedlar crying "Deplh for regs!", a little whitewashed yard.

And there's your answer, stranger, and now I'm sure you'll see
Why Belfast is the only place in all the world for me.

Bill Nesbitt

Reality

I used to think of Belfast as the only place for me,
But now it's all so different from the way it used to be.

Graffiti on a gable wall with messages of hate,
Proclaiming their allegiances to Crown or Irish State,
The sound of an explosion as it rumbles through the air,
Faces lined with signs of shock, shoulders drooped with care,
Communities divided by the barriers of strife,
Chaos and confusion and mayhem running rife,
Eyes that show the shedding of a million bitter tears,
Reflecting all the horrors, and the hardships, and the fears,
Slaughter in a crowded bar that no one can forget,
Innocents machine-gunned as they go to place a bet,
Little children orphaned as they watch their parents die,
With no one who can answer them, or give a reason why,
Soldiers at a road block, while, hanging overhead,
A helicopter hovers like a spider on a thread,
Armed police with riot shields before a frenzied mob,
Stones and bottles flying, just hazards of the job,
An Armalite that's pointed at an unsuspecting sentry,
While, somewhere, some misguided youth is knee-capped up an
    entry,
Arsonists who torch a church in wanton desecration,
Families left homeless through rank intimidation,
Incendiaries in a city store, burning jobs away,
Blackmail and extortion the order of the day,
Politicos protesting their deep dissatisfaction,
Long on wind and long on words, inadequate in action,
A people praying for a peace, with all their main and might,
A people who have wearied of the futile, fruitless fight.

And that's the dark and ugly face of Belfast that I see,
And why it isn't, any more, the only place for me.

Bill Nesbitt

The Bad Habit

An adoring Scottish mother is speaking to her son
In her tender, loving, warm, devoted way -
And I'd like you to agree
To come along with me
And to eavesdrop on the things she has to say...

    *   *   *   *   *   *

"Now, Hamish, please... don't pick your nose...
For what on earth do you suppose
The clergyman would have to say
If he should chance to pass this way?

"Son, you must take my advice -
Picking noses, isn't nice...
I really don't know why you do it -
I'm telling you, some day you'll rue it!

"You'll have to use your handkerchief,
Otherwise, you'll come to grief,
For, on the end of your wee finger,
Germs that cause infections linger...

"It really is an awful sin,
The way you shove your finger in
And don't you think you ought to hide
The sort of things you find inside?

"Now, listen, Hamish, little son -
Picking noses isn't done
Whenever people are about...
So, Hamish, take that finger out!

"It's not the proper thing to do
And very terribly non-U..
And folk who fiddle with their noses
Lose the scent of pines and roses

"It's horrible the way you linger,
Twisting, digging with your finger -
Did no-one ever tell you that
You're really quite an ill-bred brat?

"It causes me great aggravation
To see your constant excavation,
And, honestly, I just can't stick it -
So, Hamish, Hamish - please don't pick it!

"Noses, son, are made for blowing,
Not for digging or for hoeing -
And some day, you'll run out of luck
And find your finger has got stuck!

"It doesn't give me cause to grin
To see you push that finger in -
It comes out looking most unclean...
And, on the end, there's something... green...!

"They say that manners maketh man,
So kindly stop it, if you can -
It isn't pleasant to behold...
So, Hamish, why are you so bold?

"Eternally, without cessation,
You're at your nasal exploration -
You'll finish in a right schemozzle
If you keep fiddling with your nozzle!

"You'll never find yourself a wife
If you go on throughout your life
Forcing both your nostrils wide -
You'd sicken any would-be bride!

"For do you think some pretty miss
Would fancy seeing such as this?
You'd be a fine, romantic suitor...
Your finger jammed inside your hooter...

"Remember, son, you're growing up,
And not a young, uncultured pup -
But that's enough... I'll say no more...
For, after all... you're sixty-four...!"

Bill Nesbitt

The Dale

Now, they've got a reputation in Ballymena town
For savin' every ha'penny, every tanner and half-crown,
But they're very decent people, respectable and clean,
And I don't believe a word of it when people call them mean.

But there's one man in particular, whose name I'm keeping quiet,
Who's the meanest man in Ulster, and no one can deny it,
Beside his stingy manners, oul' Scrooge's deeds would pale.
And I'm sure that you will all agree when you have heard my tale.

He'd work his farm the live long day, he'd rise up at the dawn
And keep on working through the dark, long past daylight gone,
His eldest son was thirty six, his youngest twenty three,
And he kept the poor lads at it till they looked as old as he.

Well, he had a great ambition that he wanted to expand
And he had his greedy eye upon his neighbour's bit of land,
Until, one day, to his delight, that land came up for sale.
If he'd have been a spaniel, he'd have gone and wagged his tail!

So he went and saw the daler, and he haggled at the price,
And fought for every shillin' he could possibly entice,
And, after hours of wranglin', the daler made the sale,
I'd swear, he wasn't happy at his profit on the dale!

The signin' up was organised for nine o'clock next day,
And on the dot, your man arrived, says he, "How much to pay?"
"Sixty thousand, eighty nine," replied the auctioneer,
"That's the price that we agreed." Says he, "I've got it here."

His eldest son walked in the dure, a bucket in each hand,
Each one overflowin' with the coinage of the land,
Pounds and fivers, fifty pences, stuffed up to the brim,
Buckets full of money, spillin' at the rim.

He threw it on the counter for the office clerk to count,
And it took the poor lad ages, 'twas such a large amount,
But when at last he'd finished, his face was sad to see,
Says he, "I'm awful sorry, but you're short of twenty pee."

The oul' boy turned round to his son, and gave him fierce abuse,
Says he, "Ye're just an eejit, and not a pick of use!
I said to fetch the money, but when you went and tuk it
Ye acted like a gommeral, for you fetched me THE WRONG
    BUCKET!"

Bill Nesbitt

Feeling Fragile

I'm feelin' sort of fragile, and far from hale and hearty.
I must have had a smashin' time at Willie Wilson's party!
I can't mind much about it, but I must have had a ball,
For the fact is, at the moment, I don't feel good at all!

I've a sneakin' recollection of seeing Jinny Jones,
And I've got a sinkin' feelin' right down inside my bones
That I wasn't quite as sensible as might have been supposed
For, though I just can't stand her, I've a feelin' I proposed!'

The trouble is, I can't think straight, for I had a right old sup,
And boys, I'm awful worried that she went and took me up!
I just can't mind her answer, and I don't know what to do,
But one thing's sure and certain, I'm in a fair old stew.

I know I ought to phone her, but I'd get an awful fright
If I discovered what I'm fearing turns out to be right!
I cannot even write to her, for then without a doubt,
If she had it down on paper, I could never wriggle out!

Didn't I? Or did I? The answer's got me vexed.
Small wonder that I'm lookin' green, and feelin' fierce perplexed!
Have I gone and stuck my silly head inside a bridal halter?
Are my days of freedom numbered? Am I headed for the altar?

What did Jinny answer me, all those hours ago?
Oh, boys, I'd be delighted if I thought that she'd said "No!"
Just think, a drop of porter has led to my undoin',
And a glass or two of whiskey has brought me near to ruin!

Here, wait a minute... there's the phone! "Hello?... Yes, this is me."
"Oh!... Jinny.... it's yourself... well, no... I'm not exactly free...
"You want to ask a question? Well... all right... go ahead...
I'm dreading it, but - hold on, Jinny... what was that you said...?"

"You say you're feelin' fierce ashamed at what you did last night?
"You had a drop too much to drink, and passed out like a light?
"You cannot mind the things you said? And now you want to know...?
"I'm sorry! I've forgotten too... So Jinny, cheerio!"

Bill Nesbitt

The Process

Consider, if you will, with me
The act of procreation -
The task we set about, with glee,
For Man's regeneration…
And tell me, husband, tell me, wife -
This deed inspired by Cupid…
Have you ever, in your life
Seen anything more stupid?

You'd think that God, in all His wit
And mighty comprehension
Could surely have improved on it,
This singular invention -
The thought of all the human herd
Indulging in this action
Is one that strikes me as absurd -
I'm dumb with stupefaction!

It starts off with a tender kiss,
Develops into passion -
And, after that, it's hit or miss
In most haphazard fashion…
The logic in this foolish feat,
This striving and this straining,
The sweating skin, the humid heat,
Is quite beyond explaining!

They say it makes the world go round
And sends this planet spinning -
With half a chance, the thing is bound
To tempt saints into sinning,
But I am not a holy saint,
Nor am I hard to tempt,
And, from libido's lustful taint,
I'm nowhere near exempt!

It's just the same with birds and bees
And every other creature -
With fawns and frogs and flies and fleas,
Life's most compelling feature…
And yet I feel that I must say
I've reached the firm deduction -
There should have been a simpler way
Of human reproduction.

The process is uncouth and crude
And highly inefficient
(Though I have done the best I could
To make myself proficient!)…
The whole thing is a tangled mess
And very far from clever -
But yet, you know I must confess….
I wouldn't change it - ever…!

Bill Nesbitt

Hypochondriac

Now, doctor, dear doctor, you're busy, I know,
But, please, would you kindly examine my toe?
Normally, doctor, I wouldn't complain,
But you'll have to do something - I can't stand the pain...

What's that you're saying? My shoes are too tight?
A pair a size bigger will soon put me right?
I know what I'd like - if I gave a description
Do you think that, perhaps, you could write a prescription?

You can't? Well, I think that you're very unfair,
For, really, I cannot afford a new pair -
But tell me this, doctor... now that I'm here,
I wonder if, maybe, you'd look at my ear?

You tell me the problem is only with wax?
Thank you, dear doctor - that's helped me relax...
I was really annoyed at the symptoms it's showing -
Firmly convinced that my hearing was going...

Now, doctor, please tell me this - do you suppose
You could spare me a moment to look up my nose?
I reckon I might have a touch of catarrh,
And it's leaving me feeling not quite up to par...

Fair enough, doctor - you say it's a cold,
But, doctor, forgive me for being so bold
As to question an obvious expert like you...
But, doc, are you certain it isn't the 'flu?

I hope you don't think that I'm making a fuss,
But another small matter I'd like to discuss -
On the back of my hand, I've a very odd spot...
Do you think that it's something exotic I've got?

Very well, doctor, I hear what you say...
It's nothing at all, and will soon fade away...
Well, doctor, I hope and I pray that you're right,
For I'm worried in case it might grow - and it might!

Now, doctor, dear doctor, I'm not finished yet
There's another small problem, before I forget...
This morning, two pimples appeared on my bottom -
And, doctor, I haven't a clue how I got 'em....

You're telling me, doctor, there's nothing to fear?
A couple of days, and they'll both disappear?
Are you certain those pimples don't need to be treated?
Steady on, doc - there's no need to get heated....

You don't have to push me, now, doctor - I'm going...
I don't like the look of the temper you're showing -
But, doctor, dear doctor, before I go off,
I've been troubled of late by a bit of a cough....

What's this you're doing? You're throwing me out?
You're going to hear from my lawyers, no doubt...
The way that you've treated me, doc, is a crime -
So I'm going to sue you... for wasting my time...!

Bill Nesbitt

The Garden

Would you look at my dahlias, they're failures,
  and the greenfly has flummoxed my phlox.
My sunflowers stoop, my delphiniums droop,
  and something has savaged my stocks.
My willow tree's wilted and terribly tilted,
  I've made a right ass of my asters,
And though it seems crazy, even my daisies
  turn out to be downright disasters.

My anemones have their own enemies,
  my begonias are so woe-begone,
There's ants in my poor anthirrhinums,
  and masses of moss in my lawn.
My sweet peas are sour, my lobelias won't flower,
  my cornflowers suffer from bunions
And my radishes rot, my rose has black spot
  and my sage bushes don't know their onions!

I tried some chrysanths, but they're terrible plants,
  I can't seem to grow them at all.
My artichoke's croaked (by chickweed choked),
  and my wallflower's gone to the wall.
My peas haven't flowered, for they've all been devoured
  by some insect that fancies their taste,
And some little hallions have ruined my scallions,
  the whole thing's a terrible waste!

It's really too bad to see just how sad
  are the hearts of my poor gladioli.
My thyme is too tardy, and not very hardy,
  and my Honesty looks most unholy.
My runner bean's walked, and my broad beans have baulked,
  my cucumber has lost all its cool,
And my marrow's no bone, and I grumble and groan
  at the hundreds of weeds I've to pull.

My lupin's in loops, the leaves curled in hoops,
    my nasturtium's nasty to view
My savoys have all sagged, and my leeks all need lagged,
    and my daffodils don't seem to do.
My marigold's dead, for it's more mari-lead,
    as a flower it hadn't much mettle,
And my blackcurrant's bare.... and I'm going to swear,
    for I've gone and been stung by a nettle.

My beetroot are beaten, won't ever be eaten,
    my apples would give you the pip.
My Love-in-a Mist will never be kissed,
    my tulips all give me the slip.
The whole thing's a mess, and the answer, I guess,
    is to know I'm completely defeated,
And to buy some cement, for my urgent intent
    is to have the whole shambles concreted!

Bill Nesbitt

Epilogue

My thoughts are confused, and my mind is unclear,
And I'm trying to write, but the words won't appear,
And I find I'm unable to reel off a rhyme,
I tell you, I'm having a terrible time!

I'm filled with despair, and I'm fraught with frustration,
Devoid of ideas, with no inspiration,
Fuming and fretting and twirling my thumbs,
The harder I try, the worse it becomes!

I'm sure every writer and poet like me
Has suffered the same, and is bound to agree
That, when the result of their effort appears,
It's due to a torrent of blood, sweat and tears!

Whenever my mind is divorced from my brain,
With each word the product of heartache and pain,
And I'm just on the verge of admitting defeat
That's when I visit my little retreat.

It isn't palatial (I cannot deny it),
But there I find solace, and comfort and quiet.
It soothes me, it calms, it's the ultimate unction,
Though it's meant to perform a quite different function!

I've heard people state their considered belief
That the loo's only purpose is that of relief,
Relief from discomfort and bodily need,
But its purpose, for me, is quite different, indeed!

There's none to disturb me, to say "Yea" or "Nay".
I'm master and monarch of all I survey,
Shedding my cares as I perch on my throne,
My mind concentrated, my thoughts all my own.

In calm and contentment, I meditate there,
Shielded from worry, and freed from despair.
My spirits are light, and my heart is aglow
As the muse goes to work, and the verse starts to flow.

And so, you've been reading the outcome today -
You'll know that my efforts are more than mere play -
And if the result by the critics is slated,
Just think of the place where this verse was created!

Bill Nesbitt